EMOTI(

MW01225606

A PRACTICAL GUIDE TO MASTERING EMOTIONS

JONNY BELL

Copyright © 2014

Why You Should Read This Book

Do you find yourself churning in a sea of constant emotion, eternally a slave to the negative or positive feelings you hold? Do you find yourself acting out based on those emotions, negatively affecting your relationships and your work life?

Work to build better relationships, eliminate stress, and reach eternal success in your life by understanding the unique idea of emotional intelligence. Your emotional intelligence level is, arguably, far more important than you IQ; however, you can alter your emotional intelligence and build it to create a better life for yourself. Your emotional intelligence measures how well you can identify and understand your interior, unique emotions and how well you can identify and empathize with the unique emotions of others. With this understanding, you can build a more compassionate world: a world free of bullying, full of easily resolvable conflict. Are you ready to build a more emotionally intelligent world?

This book includes a quiz to allow you to understand your current, unique emotional intelligence. With your emotional intelligence level in hand, you can move forward to the step-by-step instructions on how to live your life more emotionally intelligent. You can begin to alter the ways in which you communicate; you can begin to alter the way you react to your emotions. You can eliminate the "slave" idea and its association with your emotions. You cannot control your emotions, no. Of course not. They are your personal data; they are a part of you. However, you can control yourself and your reactions to these emotions. Learn how.

Begin to meet your emotions and accept them. The idea of "hiding your feelings" from yourself is now doomed. You must commune with your interior self and get to know yourself better. And this book lends you the unique emotional intelligence history and context to allow you to understand how. Don't wait another day to fuel yourself with emotional intelligence. Beautiful relationships and enhanced successes are waiting for you.

TABLE OF CONTENTS

CHAPTER 1. EMOTIONAL INTELLIGENCE: AN OVERVIEW

Emotion holds an over-arching control on humanity. All decisions are monitored with regards to anger, happiness, boredom, or sheer frustration; how often, for example, have you chosen to watch a particular movie because you were sad? How often have you gone on vacation out of frustration for your daily "grind" lifestyle? You are a slave to your emotions. They are as much a part of you as your skeleton, as your kidneys and liver.

Your emotions are complex, psychological, involving three segments: a physiological response, a subjective experience, and an expressive, occasionally behavioral response. The subjective experience refers to the fact that people all over the world—regardless of their particular culture—experience the same basic emotions. However, these basic emotions have a highly subjective range of experience. Therefore, "sadness" means something different for everyone, besides the fact that it is a very basic human response to something upsetting.

Your physiological response is precisely what it sounds like, of course. When your stomach flutters with anxiety, when your heart beats rapidly, you are experiences physiological responses to your emotions. Research shows that the amygdala, a portion of the brain, triggers these reactions as it enacts a very big role in the formation of emotions—most notably, in the formation of fear. Your behavioral response, on the other hand, is your

1

very particular expression of your emotion. You enact your emotions and you show them "on your sleeve" so often, as the expression goes. These expressions can be universal, like a smile indicating happiness; alternately, they can be cultural. For example, in Japan, people tend to cover up their emotional fear expressions; they also tend to cover their emotional disgust expression.

This expression of emotion is precisely what emotional intelligence is concerned with. Your ability to understand other people's emotional expression is your emotional intelligence; some researchers state that your emotional intelligence is actually more important than you IQ. After all, with a proper emotional intelligence, you can interact with people from all over the world. You can parse through any conversation because you understand, essentially, what the other person is feeling. You can read them like an open book. Therefore, emotional intelligence is like a map to the world.

Four Branches of Emotional Intelligence

Peter Salovey and John D. Mayer, cultivators in the emotional intelligence research field, proposed the following four factors of emotional intelligence.

1. Perceiving Emotions

The initial step on the road to emotional intelligence is having the ability to correctly perceive emotions. This generally involves picking up on nonverbal clues like facial expression and body language and having the ability to assess what these things mean.

2. REASONING AND THINKING WITH REGARDS TO THESE EMOTIONS

This step requires the utilization of emotions in order to promote cognitive activity. Through emotions, you can begin to prioritize the things you are paying attention to; you can garner your emotions with regards to the things that gain your attention.

3. COMPREHENDING EMOTIONS

In this step, you'll look at your emotions a little closer. Each emotion carries a plethora of meaning. For example, if you see someone with angry emotions, you must understand precisely where this anger came from and what this might mean for the person and for your surroundings. If, in this example, your friend is acting angry, he could be angry with something you said last night; alternately, he could be angry because he got a speeding ticket that morning or finds himself in a fight with his girlfriend. The meaning behind different people's emotions is incredibly varied, and it's best not to jump to any conclusions. Furthermore, you must begin to comprehend your own emotions. When you feel a certain way, you must diagnose where those feelings came from. What triggers you? This can help you understand yourself a bit better.

4. MANAGING EMOTIONS

You must begin to manage and regulate your emotions. Through this, you can begin to respond appropriately to your emotions and the emotions of others. This is the true, high-level focus of emotional intelligence. You must have the ability to apply your perceptions of the world.

Measurements of Emotional Intelligence

There are several ways in which to discover your emotional intelligence; for example, there's a quick and easy quiz included in this e-book. Other emotional intelligence quizzes align themselves with the following:

1. Multifactor Emotional Intelligence Scale (MEIS)

This ability-based test asks you to perform a series of tasks; each task assess your unique ability to identify, perceive, utilize, and understand various emotions.

2. Reuven Bar-On's EQ-I

This self-report test measures your stress tolerance, your problem solving abilities, your awareness, and your general, overall happiness.

3. Seligman Attributional Style Questionnaire

This test was originally designed to be a screening test for Metropolitan Life, an insurance company. The test measures your unique levels of pessimism and optimism.

4. EMOTIONAL COMPETENCE INVENTORY

The ECI is based on the older Self-Assessment Questionnaire. This very specific inventory provides a unique "number" or "level" for each individual's competencies with regards to emotions.

UTILIZATION OF EMOTIONAL INTELLIGENCE

As you work to discover how to utilize your emotions and understand the emotions of the people around you, you can maximize your impact and happiness in many situations. At home, work, or school, you can begin to guide your relationships in a healthy manner and solve problems. In these direct compartments, you can begin to:

1. MANAGE YOUR ANGER.

How often has an argument gotten out of control because you or someone else couldn't handle the feelings of anger? Hot emotions, like jealousy or anger, can be difficult to manage. However, if you maintain a level of emotional intelligence, you can calm yourself. You can direct your mind to think about unrelated things, about funny encounters that hold no relation to the current problem. You can utilize various coping mechanisms, as well; for example, you can concentrate on the direct, realistic situation at hand rather than the emotions attached to it. Alternately, you can begin to look at the situation from another's perspective to get a full grasp of it.

2. READ BODY LANGUAGE.

Scientists state that body language subsists a full sixty percent of all communication. With proper emotional intelligence, you can begin to understand the body language of other people to operate in a world without unnecessary words. When you begin to pick up on body language cues, you can react responsibly to what a person is feeling. For example, if you notice that a person is acting especially shy or unconfident, you would not speak loudly and aggressively at that person. Instead, you'd speak slowly, kindly, in attempts to coax the person into better confidence and assuredness.

3. MANAGE YOUR EMOTIONS IN ALTERNATE SETTINGS.

With emotional intelligence in hand, it won't matter what sort of people you speak to or where, in the world, you are. You will have the ability to handle any anxiety you, personally, have about a certain situation or group of people. And as you handle your own emotions, you'll be able to face other people and help them work through their emotions by understanding them and having compassion.

4. HOLD BETTER TEAM RECRUITMENT AND SELECTION SKILLS.

With emotional intelligence, you can begin to work as a better team leader or manager. Many team leaders utilize emotional intelligence in order to select new candidates to be a part of the team. They work to find new candidates who can manage their own emotions; candidates who can develop strong relationships that enhance productivity and improve performance.

5. *TRAIN AND COACH EFFICIENTLY.*

Emotional intelligence is utilized to build better skills throughout a team. Coaches or trainers are able to conduct emotional intelligence assessments to recognize team training needs. They develop team training content to hone specific training needs for overall team productivity.

6. *CREATE STUDENT ASSESSMENTS.*

Emotional intelligence is further utilized to create student assessments in various educational institutions; these assessments predict student performances. The assessment tools allow teaches to utilize these predictions to build improvements and boost future performances.

7. *EFFECT TEAM BUILDING.*

Emotional intelligence creates an in-depth relationship across a broad team of individuals. Each person in a team has specific strengths and weaknesses that can be maximized utilizing emotional intelligence; this, in turn, can maximize team productivity.

Chapter 2. History of Emotional Intelligence

Initial construction of emotional intelligence is found in the 1930's. A man named Edward Thorndike described social intelligence as a concept that involves the ability one has to co-habitat with other people. Twenty years later, Abraham Maslow, a humanistic psychologist, lent a description about how people can build proper emotional strength. He was the architect of the Maslow Hierarchy; he stated that one must have food and shelter and safety prior to achieving good mental and emotional abilities. He stressed the fact that people must have other people with which they can commune and reside.

1983 brought Howard Gardner's Frames of Mind: The Theory of Multiple intelligences. This paper constructed the idea that the traditional formation of "intelligence" measurement, the IQ reading, didn't fully initiate the grand scheme of cognitive ability. Gardner's idea was about multiple intelligences: both interpersonal intelligence and intrapersonal intelligence. Interpersonal intelligence, in this instance, is the ability to understand the motivations and intentions of exterior people. Intrapersonal intelligence, on the other hand, is the ability to understand and appreciate your own emotions and motivations.

The first mention of the term "emotional intelligence" bounced to view in 1985. A graduate student named Wayne Leon Payne first formulated the term. It took a good five years after this initial "term paper" for the phrase emotional intelligence to burst forth. But it most certainly did.

In 1990, two American professors named Peter Salovey and John Mayer were published in two academic jounrals. Mayer of the University of New Hampshire and Salovey of Yale University were both interested in scientifically understanding the grand difference between people's perception of emotions. They both understood that some people had greater understanding and identification techniques with regards to their own emotions and the emotions of others; furthermore, they were much more able to solve emotion problems.

Daniel Goleman and his Mixed Model of Emotions

1995 brought best-selling Emotional Intelligence: Why It Can Matter More than IQ by Daniel Goleman. Daniel Goleman developed on Mayer and Salovey's work. He stated that most of people's success in their lives is determined by their emotional intelligence; he stated this in direct contrast to the common view that cognitive intelligence is the great determining factor in terms of success. He described intelligent people as people who can understand and manage their emotions; as people who are empathetic to the emotional drives of other people.

Goleman introduced the Mixed Model of Emotional Intelligence. His model issues a plethora of skills that push leadership performance in various stages. The

Emotional Intelligence
following are the four stages:

1. *SELF-REGULATION*

According to Goleman, controlling your disruptive, chaotic emotions and impulses and having the ability to adapt to altering circumstances is incredibly important in terms of emotional intelligence.

2. *SELF-AWARENESS*

Having the ability to understand your strengths, weaknesses, motivators, values, and goals in terms of your overall emotions promotes emotional intelligence. He states that you must recognize the impact your emotions have on others, and you have the ability to utilize your gut feelings to guide your over-arching decisions.

3. *SOCIAL SKILL*

You are able to manage your relationships with your unique ability to control your emotions and understand and empathize with the emotions of others. Through this managing of your relationships, you are able to "move" people to the decision or direction you require. For example, you are able to stop fights and arguments by reasoning and understanding the other person's emotions.

4. *MOTIVATION.*

You are driven by an interior motivation—not by an

exterior motivation. You want to achieve for your own sake of achieving. This, as Goleman states, is incredibly important for leadership; if you don't care, how do you expect your team members beneath you to respond?

5. EMPATHY.

When you are making decisions as a leader, you are meant to continually consider other people's feelings and emotions. Because you have emotional intelligence, you can see and actually feel their emotions; you can make any and all decisions based on this understanding.

CHAPTER 3. EMOTIONAL INTELLIGENCE QUIZ: UNDERSTANDING YOUR EMOTIONAL INTELLIGENCE LEVEL

Take the following quiz in order to take a self-evaluation of your specific emotional intelligence. With this information in mind, you can begin to strengthen your emotional intelligence and further your ranks in the world.

QUESTION 1: IN MY GENERAL GROUP OF PEERS, I USUALLY UNDERSTAND HOW EVERY PERSON AROUND ME FEELS ABOUT EVERY OTHER PERSON IN THE SAME SOCIAL GROUP.

A. Strongly Agree
B. Agree
C. Disagree
D. Strongly Disagree

QUESTION 2: WHEN I'M ANGRY OR UPSET IN SOME WAY, I CAN USUALLY DIAGNOSE THE REASON FOR MY DISTRESS.

A. Strongly Agree
B. Agree
C. Disagree
D. Strongly Disagree

QUESTION 3: OF COURSE I KNOW I HAVE SOME IMPROVEMENTS TO MAKE IN SOME AREAS; HOWEVER, I GENERALLY LIKE MYSELF.

A. Strongly Agree
B. Agree
C. Disagree
D. Strongly Disagree

QUESTION 4: WHEN I ACCIDENTALLY MAKE A MISTAKE, I
USUALLY CRITICIZE MYSELF AND PUT MYSELF DOWN.

A. Almost Never
B. Rarely
C. Sometimes
D. Often

QUESTION 5: I AM UNCOMFORTABLE WHEN THE CURRENT
SITUATION IS TENSE OR OTHERWISE EMOTIONALLY-CHARGED.

A. Strongly Agree
B. Agree
C. Disagree
D. Strongly Disagree

QUESTION 6: I AVOID ARGUMENTS AND CONFRONTATION AT ALL
COST. DURING ARGUMENTS, I BECOME FRAZZLED AND ANXIOUS.

A. Strongly Agree
B. Agree
C. Disagree
D. Strongly Disagree

7. I TEND TO KEEP MY DISTANCE FROM PEOPLE UNTIL I REALLY
GET TO KNOW THEM. PEOPLE COULD SAY I CAN BE ALOOF.

Emotional Intelligence

A. Strongly Agree

B. Agree

C. Disagree

D. Strongly Disagree

8. *I OFTEN OVERREACT TO MINISCULE PROBLEMS IN MY LIFE.*

A. Almost Never

B. Rarely

C. Sometimes

D. Often

9. *I AM CONFIDENT ABOUT MY TALENTS AND ABILITIES. I HAVE STRONG SKILLS IN DESIGNATED AREAS.*

A. Strongly Agree

B. Agree

C. Disagree

D. Strongly Disagree

10. *I ABSOLUTELY AM A GOOD JUDGE OF PEOPLE'S CHARACTER.*

A. Strongly Agree

B. Agree

C. Disagree

D. Strongly Disagree

11. *UNPLEASANT TASKS MAKE ME:*

A. Work through a little bit of a plan every single day.

B. Finish the task as soon as I can.

C. Procrastinate and finish at the very last minute.

D. Write it off and don't do it.

14

12. AN ARGUMENT MAKES ME:

A. Quit fighting and agree to take a brief break from the discussion to cool down.
B. Completely shut down and stop any sort of response.
C. End the discussion rapidly with an apology.
D. Bring insults to the table.

13. IMPORTANT DECISIONS BRING ME TO:

A. Align my decision with my instincts.
B. Ask for advice and rely on that advice.
C. Opt for the easy way out.
D. Take a guess.

14. PICK ONE OF THE FOLLOWING STATEMENTS TO DESCRIBE YOURSELF:

A. I make friends easily and get to know people well instinctively.
B. I have a great companionship quality to me; however, I have to really know someone prior to naming them my actual friend.
C. I don't think it's very easy to make new friends.
D. I simply cannot meet people or make friends.

15. YOU'VE BROUGHT BOUNDLESS ENERGY TO A CLASS PROJECT, AND YET YOU FIND YOURSELF RECEIVING A C. WHAT WOULD YOUR THOUGHTS BE?

A. I would consider the different ways I could improve the project; I would bring these thoughts to additional

school work.
B. I would ask the professor for a different grade, utilizing reason to persuade him or her.
C. I would criticize my work, making myself feel worse.
D. I would quit putting effort and energy into the class because the class is stupid.

16. SUDDENLY, YOU FEEL AS IF YOU HAVE TOO MANY PROJECTS BEFORE YOU. HOW DO YOU FEEL?

A. You are anxious about getting everything done, of course.
B. You are completely overwhelmed.
C. You are angry that your boss has allowed you to become so overworked.
D. You are depressed, understanding fully that you'll never finish everything.

Your Results

If you answered mostly A's, you have a wonderful emotional intelligence. You are able to interact with people and understand their needs. You are able, for example, to give them the space they require and the support they need during hard times. Furthermore, you are able to understand your interior emotions and how to better your feelings in order to work constructively.

If you answered mostly B's and C's, you have average emotional intelligence. You are generally good at understanding and acting upon your emotions. However, you are only moderately comfortable with emotional and social conflicts. Furthermore, you have trouble expressing your feelings. Consider the questions you most struggled with above, and take stock of yourself. How can you improve your emotional intelligence?

If you answered mostly D's, on the other hand, your emotional intelligence has a lot of room for improvement. You are generally unable to deal with social situations; you find yourself filled with self-doubt. You also cannot grapple with your particular feelings about certain subjects. You cannot grow and move forward to a healthy environment.

Chapter 4. Emotional Intelligence Methods and Techniques

The Six Seconds Model

The Six Seconds Model provides a framework for accessing and utilizing emotions effectively. This action-oriented model provides a significant boost in productivity, as mentioned in the McDonald's case study in the previous chapter.

Six Seconds developed the model in 1997 to lend assistance with the utilization of emotions in everyday life. The model revs the three following ideas forward: the idea of becoming more aware of what you and others do, the idea of becoming more intentioned with everything you do, and the idea of becoming more purposeful and doing each action for a reason. According to Six Seconds, this creates an immense boost in productivity; perhaps this is because people feel like their life is being lived for a purpose

1. Know Yourself.

This section initiates the fact that you must be much more aware of yourself. As you clearly understand how you feel and how your feelings interact with what you do, you'll become closer to yourself. You must begin to think of your emotions as your data; you must begin to collect the information in order to make a sort of commitment to understanding who you are. Sure you're a person and you have many idiosyncrasies; you might not always understand why you do the things you do. But there are almost always a few consistent links in the chain of your life. Begin to notice them.

2. CHOOSE YOURSELF.

This section reiterates that you must do what you mean to do; therefore, you must become more intentioned with your actions. You no longer act on a sort of "autopilot." For example, instead of reacting out of anger and sending a nasty remark back to someone who angered you, you say something intentioned. You say something that creates meaning. You do not create anger for not reason with your actions. Each of your actions are proactive and well-formulated in your brain.

3. GIVE YOURSELF.

This section maximizes the purposes of your actions. You have a mission, a goal in your life. Everyone does—even if they haven't discovered it yet. By knowing yourself and analyzing your life goals and by "choosing yourself" by placing intention on your actions, you'll begin to do everything in your life for a reason. You can lead a life full of purpose, full of integrity.

VITAL SIGNS MODEL

The Vital Signs model of emotional intelligence defines performance as a people-driven, action-oriented result. It brings a framework to fuel team leadership and highly efficient teams and organizations.

VITAL SIGNS PERFORMANCE

According to the Vital Signs model, each high performing team, organization, or individual leader balances the following ideas:

1. Strategy: A clear, complete path and direction going forward; one is fueled with a Strategy.
2. Operations: The clear path and direction is enacted upon; one is fueled with action Operations.
3. Organization: Each operation maintains a series of separate systems and intricate focuses; it brings a high sense of organization to the strategy.
4. People: Each operation is fueled with the idea that they must support the very people who create the action.

According to the Vidal Signs Model, there must be an intricate balance between people and organization, and an intricate balance between strategy and operations. Sometimes, of course, an organization must fuel their energy toward a particular segment during a specific period of time. For example, if a team must focus more on the operation side of things during a product-launch, that's okay; however, if this operation is focused on for too long, the organization will begin to lose sight of their desired direction and strategy they proclaimed at the very beginning of the organization formation.

VITAL SIGNS WORKPLACE CLIMATE

According to this model, the workplace climate is very

important with regards to allowing the people to work in optimal, efficient measures. Climate drives work performance immensely and, unlike culture, it can be changed rather rapidly. For example, you would much rather invest your time and energy in a place you feel safe and happy in; you wouldn't want to work in an arena of toxicity.

1. Trust: The workplace climate requires a good deal of trust. People must feel safe and assured in their workplace; this feeling of safety allows them to innovate and take risks. Innovation only formulates with steps outside comfort zones.

2. Motivation: People must feel the commitment and energy to work beyond the minimum measures. In turn, the energy and drive they enact will rev the company or organization's performance forward.

3. Change: People must have the ability to continually innovate and alter themselves and their surroundings. They can do this with greater emotional intelligence; they can understand, for example, how their co-worker is feeling and lower their voice to become more compassionate and considerate toward their co-worker. They must be continually adaptable to changing workplace rules, as well, as the company begins to attempt greater feats.

4. Teamwork: People must feel the communication energy and the collaborate energy in a workplace. Therefore, they must feel like they are a part of something—something they truly care about—in order

to put their maximum work effort forward. Think about this: you are much more likely to go running in the morning if you know someone is waiting for you outside your door, waiting for you to go running with him. If you are consistently answering to someone—someone with similar interests—then you will put your best effort forward.

5. Execution: People at the company must be focused on their actions and accountable for their actions. Therefore, if they make a mistake, they must understand their mistake and become focused on not creating that mistake again.

According to research on the Vital Signs Model, at least sixty percent of all performance is determined by the strength and vitality of the climate.

.

CHAPTER 5. SHARPEN YOUR EMOTIONAL INTELLIGENCE

Begin to tap into your emotions and the emotions of others and utilize this ability to build a better, more communicative life for yourself. Manage your stress levels and enhance your life continually. Your emotional intelligence level, as found in the previous chapter, is not like your IQ. Your IQ remains constant during your life, while emotional intelligence can build continually. Utilize the following techniques to hone your emotional intelligence today.

GET IN TOUCH WITH YOUR EMOTIONS

1. MAKE A LIST OF ALL OF YOUR EMOTIONAL REACTIONS YOU EXPERIENCE THROUGHOUT YOUR DAY.

Usually, you put your emotions on the "backburner." You don't allow them to influence you; you try to ignore them, if you can. During this new day of emotional intelligence, however, you must begin to acknowledge how your emotions change during each experience. These emotions are important facets of the data you collect about yourself.

After something occurs in your day, like you feel angry at a work meeting because someone cut you off, go back to your desk and write what happened and how you felt about it. Alternately, if you feel good after a dinner date with a good friend, go back to your house and write about it. Every experience alters your emotions readily;

it's your job to notice it. Try noticing your emotions throughout your everyday at specific times. How, for example, do you usually feel when you wake up? How do you feel in the minutes before you fall asleep?

2. LISTEN TO YOUR BODY.

Don't ignore how your body reacts to your emotions. Your mind and your body are a cohesive machine, and everything you think and feel intensely alters your physical body. Read your physical cues. For example, if you have slow, lethargic limbs, you might have feelings of sadness. If you have intense energy, you might be feeling joy. If you have a tight chest, you might be stressed. Begin to read your body in order to read your interior emotions.

3. OBSERVE HOW YOUR BEHAVIOR AND YOUR EMOTIONS ARE LINKED.

Pay attention to how you react to your strong emotions. When you face certain everyday situations, try to listen to precisely what your gut is saying about them. How do you react when you listen to your emotions, rather than simply reacting without thinking? This is a list of some common examples of behaviors and their emotional link:

A. You feel angry and you raise your voice or stomp your feet.
B. You feel embarrassed and you withdraw from communication.
C. You feel overwhelmed and you completely panic, losing track of everything in your immediate situation.

4. Stop Judging Your Emotions or Why You Have Them.

All your emotions, your positive emotions and your negative emotions, are valid. Don't judge your emotions. If you do, you'll essentially be "plugging" your ability to feel. You'll be unable to utilize your emotions to enact positively. Your emotions are new pieces of data about the surrounding world. In order to stop judging your emotions, do the following;

A. Allow yourself to feel a negative emotion. Everyone has something negative within. Allow this emotion to come to the surface and connect it to the situation it aligns with. For example, if you're feeling jealous, what is that telling you about your current environment and situation?
B. Allow yourself to feel a positive emotion. Connect this joy to the environment and the situation. Learn how to connect this feeling more often in order to appreciate the world around you.

5. Note Patterns From Your Past Emotions.

Learn about how your past emotions are connected to your past experiences. When you feel something immensely strong inside yourself, connect that feeling to something you felt in the past. What happened, what occurred, in relation to that feeling?

A. When you note these patterns, you can control your future behavior. Note if you handled the situation well before, and attempt to alter it now for the better. You can

learn from your past link of emotions and actions.
B. Begin writing down your emotions and how you react to your emotions so that you can note any trends in your reactions.

6. BEGIN DECIDING HOW YOU WANT TO BEHAVE.

You can't help your emotions. They are your interior reactions. However, you can decide how you react to your emotions. If you're usually apt to act out in anger, think about the ways in which you could react and not get yourself in a bad situation.

A. When you experience something negative in your life, feel your emotions completely. But don't get swept away with them. After the initial wave of emotion, decide precisely how you'd like to behave. Communicate with these feelings; don't dispute them. Rise above them.
B. Don't tamp down your feelings or try to escape them. If your bad feelings tend to make you drink alcohol or eat too much food, try to deal with your emotions. If you turn to "escapes" too often, you won't build a better emotional intelligence.

PUT YOUR EMOTIONAL INTELLIGENCE TO GOOD USE IN THE REAL WORLD

1. ASSESS YOUR LIFE AND FIND PLACES YOU'D LIKE TO IMPROVE.

With greater emotional intelligence, you can build better relationships and work for brighter job opportunities. The following four elements, as aforementioned, can help you assess your life and find balance in your everyday life.

A. Self-awareness. Self-awareness, awareness of your overall emotions and their origins is incredibly important. You can recognize your own limitations; you can further recognize your strengths.

B. Self-management. Self-management allows you to balance your needs with the needs of your peers. You can pull back against your desire for impulse decisions. You can begin to cope with adaptations and stay committed to various projects.

C. Social awareness. Social awareness allows you to become in-tune with your peers' emotions. You can pick up on social cues and begin to understand the unique dynamics of a particular situation. You can work well in a team because you can see all parties operating individually.

D. Relationship Management. Relationship management allows you to get along with your peers and influence people to illustrate their emotions well in conversation. You can manage conflict and eliminate disruption.

2. INCREASE YOUR EMOTIONAL INTELLIGENCE AND DECREASE YOUR STRESS LEVELS.

When you feel overwhelmed by life situations, you can begin to eliminate these unnecessary feelings by orchestrating a plan to relieve yourself.

A. Understand what, in your environment and schedule, triggers your stress. When you understand that, ask yourself what in the world helps you relieve your stress. Write down a list of everything in the world that helps you decrease your stress levels. These can be simple things: reading a book, taking a walk, or playing with a dog.

B. Look to outside help, if necessary. If you're unable to deal with your stress alone, look to a psychologist or therapist who can both help you raise your emotional intelligence levels and teach you how to cope with your stressful emotions.

3. FIND WAYS TO BE MORE LIGHT-HEARTED.

Try to be optimistic in all areas of your life. With optimism, you are able to see the beauty of the world, of little, small objects. You are further able to spread these feelings of joy to your exterior peers. Remember that your peers want to be around optimistic people; they want to be drawn to the possibilities you see before you.

A. Remember that negativity forces you to focus on what can go wrong. Everything can go wrong all the time, but it's best not to focus on that. Instead, build a resilience to the chaos of the world.

B. Emotionally intelligent people can utilize humor and fun to feel safe and bring that safe happiness to their peers. Try to get out in the world and laugh a little more.

EMOTIONAL INTELLIGENCE AND DECISION-MAKING

When you hold the strength not to be influenced by your current emotions, your current feelings, you have a much greater ability to make better decisions.

Think about how often your emotions influence things that hold no relation to them. For example, when you drive to work, you're frustrated. You feel the anger and heat from the long car ride, through traffic, and you bring those emotions into your workplace. The anger you felt in your car could make you quibble with your co-worker, thus bringing a halt to your cooperation and forward-motion for the day. Alternately, you could take risks in areas you don't feel ready to take risks in, just because you feel really wonderful from something unrelated that happened the day before. You are unable to channel and live above your emotions, and your life turns chaotic as a result.

CHAPTER 6. BULLYING AND EMOTIONAL INTELLIGENCE: PREVENTATIVE MEASURES

Emotions are the root of school-related issues. Children with hopeless emotions, jealous emotions, anxious emotions—children who are, in essence, human, have a plethora of at-school problems. They have difficulty making decisions and focusing in the classroom; above all, they have difficulty building personal relationships.

Emotions are at the central core of bullying. Because about a third of all children report being bullied—and certainly there are many more who do not report—this is a serious public-health issue in schools. The bullying can turn to verbal abuse, physical aggression, or ostracism. However, at the very base of these disturbances lies a sheer lack of self-regulation and emotional understanding.

BULLYING: ADVERSE EMOTIONAL EFFECTS

Children who are bullied are at risk for serious anxiety, depression, and ideas of suicide. Furthermore, the children who enact the bullying are at risk for anxiety, depression, and increased feelings of hostility moving forward. The people who aren't bullied or do any bullying are even at risk. Research shows that bystanders are at risk for insecurity and hopelessness. Everyone in the bully triangle of victim, bully, and bystander has poor school attendance and does not idealize education in any way.

Bullying prevention throughout the United States is on the rise. Despite the fact that the nation has spent billions of dollars on the anti-bullying crusade, bullying has not declined. This is because the programs do not address the under-the-surface causes of bullying; they simply address symptoms.

EMOTIONAL INTELLIGENCE IN SCHOOLS

Emotional intelligence must be introduced in schools to eliminate bullying. The current "law" wielding does absolutely nothing; it punishes without fixing the problem. With emotional intelligence in their curriculum, children will not turn to "picking on" their peers as often; and with emotional intelligence, those being bullied will have the ability to handle the intense anxiety they feel with regards to their current bullying situation. Furthermore, they'll have the ability to get support.

Emotional intelligence can be taught just like reading or math class. With its introduction, research shows that school climate dramatically improves; classroom instruction is far more relevant. However, adults—not just children—must experience the emotional intelligence training as well in order to maximize results.

Current teacher training does not emphasize formal understanding of how to apply emotional sciences to the classroom. It does not address how to engage students to model self-regulations. Therefore, students cannot be expected to learn without the proper authority of the teacher.

RULER

Yale Center for Emotional Intelligence recently developed a program to integrate emotional intelligence into schools. The program, RULER, addresses the skills the students require to understand, recognize, label, and express their emotions. To date, RULER has assisted a full five hundred schools. The program integrates a language of emotion into every vessel of a day of instruction. Therefore, it allows this understanding of emotions to be addressed and casually integrated into the everyday environment. Furthermore, the program provides immense support for professional adults in the learning community.

One of the steps in the program requires the school to write a charter that addresses the emotional intelligence of the school system. Therefore, the charter states how the school wants to build a supportive, emotion-accepting community. How, the charter asks, can we—the community—articulate emotions and work to manage any conflict or unwanted feelings? A second step in the program allows the school to "gage its mood." Therefore, everyone can gage their precise feelings throughout each school day and build a self-awareness.

Research states that children in RULER-operated schools are less anxious; they experience less depression. They have better abilities to problem solve, and they have excellent schoolroom climates.

Avoiding the emotional intelligence building of children all over the country is a serious misstep. It risks mental illness and serious self-esteem issues. Children must understand the ways in which they feel and how to label these emotions. This way, they don't have to reach out and attack other children in order to "deal with" their emotions; they don't have to feel angry about something someone said and then create more and more victims down the line.

The children and teachers must integrate emotional intelligence into their school lives to create a stunning environment, rich with vibrant education.

ACTIVITIES TO HELP CHILDREN DEVELOP EMOTIONAL INTELLIGENCE

Work a little bit at home with your child, if you like, with the following activities. Allow your child to understand that his or her emotions are his or her own, that your child must control them and accept them. Your child was building an emotional vocabulary even in the years before she or he could talk. The following exercises build a verbal emotional vocabulary, one that your child can utilize to describe emotions and events.

Developing this "cue-reading" and socially-appropriate action is not innate. Children learn emotional intelligence through social interaction or through what you teach them.

Lending your child the ability to fuel emotional intelligence can assist them in their later friendship buildings, in their later career.

1. LONG LIST OF FEELINGS.

Get out a huge piece of paper and a colorful marker. Sit with your child and ask your child to brainstorm all the "feeling" words he or she can think of. You can help, as well. As you make the list, draw a "feeling face" next to the feeling word so that your child can recognize the feeling in two ways: both vocally and visually. As you write each word, talk about what each word means to familiarize your child with the emotion. You can teach them new words, and you can talk about ones they already know, as well.

2. LONG LIST OF FEELING NOISES.

After you create your long list of feelings and long list of feeling pictures, associate the sounds that go alongside the words, as well. Your child might not always know the word for something; but your child will probably understand the sound that aligns with it. For example, your child probably doesn't know "frustrated;" however, he probably knows "grr" in relation to the feelings.

3. KEEP READING.

Feelings are found in every story—even stories that aren't meant to be "educational emotional stories." Pick up a story that has an empathetic character that your child really appreciates. Walk your child through the story, and ask your child what the main character is feeling at particular story points. Utilize the pictures to help your child remember the words.

4. PLAY EMOTIONAL CHARADES.

Who doesn't love charades? Play with your child, and help them understand new emotional vocabulary, as well. You will pick a simple word for your child, an emotion word, that your child must act out utilize either the entire body or the face. If your child is having a rough time diagnosing her facial or body features, stand in front of a mirror so that he or she can notice what she looks like.

5. IF YOU'RE EMOTIONAL AND YOU KNOW IT SONG.

You know "If you're happy and you know it" right? Well, this time when you sing the song with your child, try to find new words to sing about. Try this one: "If you're worried and you know it, say 'uh oh.'"

6. KEEP A JOURNAL WITH YOUR CHILD.

If your child is old enough, you should suggest that he or she writes in a journal to keep track of what he or she is feeling. It can either be secret or a shared journal with you. However, it's important that your child begin to associate various words with specific feelings.

7. MAKE A COLLAGE.

For the collage activity, you'll give your child a list of four or five emotions. Next, you'll give him or her some old magazines, some scissors, some glue, and a piece of paper to make the collage on. You'll ask her to find the emotions displayed on faces in the magazine. She is then to cut them out and paste them on the piece of paper. Afterwards, she will label each face with the designated emotion.

8. ROLE PLAY.

Create a narrative with your child to bring a realistic sense to these emotional activities. Create a scenario that your child might experience at school. For example, tell your child she "can't sit with you at lunch," and ask how your child might feel when she hears this. Ask your child how she might react. When she does "react" to this with you, she'll be able to understand if she reacted well or if she reacted poorly.

Chapter 7. Emotional Intelligence and Stress Reduction

Rapidly reduce your levels of stress utilizing enhanced emotional intelligence skills. Stress can elevate your lack of control over your situation. When you are unable to handle your emotions correctly, you can begin to let your stress take hold of you. Of course, brief bouts of stress are important. Stress brings a hormone called cortisol into your blood stream; cortisol is known as the fight or flight hormone. Therefore, every time your ancestor ran away from a predator some thousand years ago, cortisol was pulsing in his veins. Similarly, every time you have to do a work presentation or some sort of race, you are fueled with motivation and, of course, that mighty hormone—cortisol.

However, stress can build up over time. It is meant to fizzle; unfortunately, this high-stress society in which we reside warrants continued bouts of stress. When cortisol builds in your veins, it begins to destroy you. For example, cortisol works like a free radical and kills brain cells—in particular, brain cells in your hippocampus. Your hippocampus is responsible for creating new brain cells; it further works to transfer short-term memories to long term memories. When your hippocampus begins to break down, you cannot work at your highest efficiency. Furthermore, a high level of cortisol reduces your metabolism, thus making you gain weight and not process food correctly. To put it simply: cortisol and stress cannot continue to ruin you.

SKILL NUMBER ONE: REDUCE STRESS QUICKLY

When you're "in the moment," fueled with a sense of stress and dread, you might not have the ability to read a situation correctly. You might not have the ability to be aware of your feelings or the needs of others. Frankly, your communicative abilities begin to falter. When you can reduce your stress dramatically in the moment, you can begin to read the situation and act emotionally correct. You can act with intention instead of with regards to your stressful emotions.

Do the following three steps in the crazy heat of a stressful moment:

1. REALIZE YOU'RE STRESSFUL FEELINGS.

This first step forces you to realize your stress levels and understand how your body reacts. For example, do your stomach muscles tighten? Are you breathing quickly? Are your hands in tight fists? When you begin to understand when you're stressed, you'll have the ability to identify it next time. You'll have the ability to begin to regulate your stress even at the helm.

2. IDENTIFY HOW YOU RESPOND TO STRESS.

You probably know that everyone's reaction to stressful situations is different. For example, if you react angrily under stress, you might look to stress-reliving events immediately after the encounter. You might go to a park and do some meditation; you might listen to calming music. Alternately, if you become withdrawn or a bit depressed in the event of stressful situations, you might look to stimulating activities immediately after your stressful encounter. You might go for a run or go to a concert.

3. DISCOVER THE AFTER-EVENT STRESS-ELIMINATING ACTIVITY OR TECHNIQUE FOR YOU.

In the hours after your stressful activity, you must engage at least one—or all—of your senses: your sense of smell, taste, sound, sight, or touch. You must find things, as aforementioned, that are either soothing or stimulating to your frame of mind. Find the precise thing that works for you, and dwell in the emotions you feel as you create your either stimulating or soothing environment.

SKILL NUMBER TWO: ELIMINATE RELATIONSHIP-ORIENTED STRESS

Understanding your emotion in each section of your life can assist you in creating proper thoughts and actions; you can remain calm and orient yourself in all tense situations with other people you may or may not have a relationship with. You can begin to communicate with other people in the most effective manner; you can allow them to understand your precise emotions while also understanding their emotions. With proper emotional intelligence, you can eliminate overwhelming feelings and look at all situations realistically.

ASK YOURSELF THE FOLLOWING QUESTIONS TO IDENTIFY YOUR RELATIONSHIP WITH YOUR EMOTIONS

1. Do your emotions find themselves accompanied by intricate, physical sensations? For example, when you're angry, do you feel it in your stomach? Alternately, when you're happy, do you feel it in your chest?

2. Are your emotions in a sort of flow? For example, do you experience one emotion after another emotion in a sort of string of emotions?

3. Do you occasionally hold intense feelings? Are these feelings hefty enough to capture the attention of both yourself and your peers?

4. Do you have discrete emotions and feelings? These feelings can be sadness, anger, joy, fear; each of these feelings can be displayed in small, discrete facial expressions.

5. Do your emotions factor into the way you make your decisions?

If you find yourself not holding familiarity with any of the past questions, you might have dulled or "turned off" emotions. To be emotionally healthy, emotionally intelligent, you must begin to accept and tune into your interior emotions. You must accept these core emotions and become comfortable with who you are in the world.

CHAPTER 8. EMOTIONAL INTELLIGENCE AND RELATIONSHIPS

You can utilize your enhanced emotional intelligence in order to build stronger relationships with your peers. Remember that laughter, humor, and play—life's natural antidotes—lighten all difficulties. They assist you in keeping everything in perspective. If you bring this lightness and energy into your relationships, you will begin to see a difference in the ways in which your communication goes. When you bring light-hearted energy into conversations, you can actually guide the other person—as long as you understand how that other person is feeling, as well. Look to the following techniques to enhance your relationships utilizing emotional intelligence.

ENACT PLAYFUL COMMUNICATION

Enacting playful communication can build your emotional intelligence; it can further help you do the following:

1. ERASE OR OTHERWISE IGNORE ALL DIFFERENCES BETWEEN YOU AND YOUR PEERS.

When you utilize playful humor, you can begin to say things to guide the conversation that have otherwise been difficult. These otherwise difficult things may have otherwise created a divide in your conversation; however, with a playful perspective, you can reach across

41

all boundaries.

2. STRIDE THROUGH HARDSHIPS.

When you can view your disappointments and difficulties with a brand new perspective, you can survive anything. Truly. You can laugh and play and eliminate depressive feelings with regards to any hardships.

3. BUILD CREATIVITY.

As you build playfulness and laughter in your life, you can free yourself of terse language and boundaries. You can begin to see things in new ways and fuel your creativity with regards to the ways in which you see every item in the world.

4. ENERGIZE AND ALSO RELAX YOUR MIND AND BODY.

As you playfully communicate and laugh, you'll relieve yourself of fatigue and also begin to relax your body. Relaxing your body further allows you to rejuvenate and accomplish more tasks in the days ahead.

HOW TO BUILD PLAYFUL COMMUNICATION

1. Begin with practice. Practice your playful communication with little kids, babies, dogs and cats, or other outgoing people who appreciate playfulness. As you begin to loosen up, you'll see the beautiful ways in which these people and animals see the world.

2. Set aside quality, regular playtime. Of course it seems

strange to "set aside" and schedule time to "play." However, it's necessary in your already cram-packed schedule. Look to have at least a little playtime every single day. When you find yourself joking and playing at least once a day, you'll become better at it. You'll find it easy to be playfully communicative.

3. Search for playful, enjoyable activities—with or without people. As you find things that assist you in loosening up and enjoying your life, you'll begin to embrace your playful emotions.

BRING PROACTIVE RESOLUTION TO RELATIONSHIP CONFLICTS

Because two people are inherently different, conflicts arise in all relationships. People have different expectations, different opinions. And this isn't a bad thing. After all, people are fueled by their individuality; it's the very thing that allows the world to revolve. It's the very thing that brings creativity and interest to the surrounding world.

However, it's best to always resolve relationship conflict in a healthy way. This healthy, constructive resolution can actually build trust between two people. With conflict—and an easy resolution at hand—a relationship can build creativity and freedom. With the ability to build a healthy resolution, you can find true safety in your relationships.

RESOLVE CONFLICT AND BUILD TRUST

43

1. CHOOSE YOUR ARGUMENTS.

Remember that working toward resolutions takes a great deal of time—especially if you're working to resolve the argument in a proactive, positive way. Consider which arguments you'd like to begin and which ones you'd like to leave off the table.

2. STAY PRESENT. STAY FOCUSED.

Let go of any past arguments and any past resentments. When you allow yourself to let go of everything else, you can realize the reality of your current argument and current situation. You can utilize this new, current situation as a platform to resolve all past conflicts.

3. END ALL UN-RESOLVABLE CONFLICTS.

Conflicts and arguments can't go on forever. If you find yourself revolving around the same argument, over and over again, you can choose to end and walk away from the conflict. Think of the expression: "Agree to disagree." Understand that everyone has different opinions and different perspectives. This should bring you peace.

4. FORGIVE THE OTHER PERSON AND YOURSELF.

Everything people have done to hurt you happened in the past. You must release your urge to punish other people; you must release the urge to seek revenge. Because of your enhanced emotional intelligence, you can have empathy for other people's perspective and feelings in those moments when they hurt you. You can rev yourself to a better future with forgiveness.

WORK TO BUILD CONNECTIONS WITH PEOPLE

1. BEGIN TO FEEL AGREEABLE AND OPEN-MINDED ABOUT THE WORLD AND ABOUT OTHER PEOPLE.

A narrow, small-minded individual unable to see other perspectives has a generally low emotional intelligence. When you have an open mind, pulsing with internal reflection, you can begin to deal with person-to-person conflicts more calmly.

A. Begin listening to debates on the radio or the television. Analyze both sides of the arguments and consider each subtlety. Remember that each side of the argument has very intricate pieces to it that require inspection.

B. When you're speaking to someone and notice they do not react "emotionally" like you normally do, try to understand why they would act differently. Try to see their emotions from their perspective.

2. BOOST YOUR EMPATHETIC FEELINGS.

When you can notice how other people are feeling and you can feel those some emotions, you are practicing empathy. You can build this skill by really listening and understanding what people are saying to you; you can further utilize this information to build better decision-making abilities.

A. Try to put yourself in other people's shoes. Think about a very specific situation in which someone currently resides. Try to imagine every element and how that would affect your feelings. Imagine how you could help alleviate any of their negative feelings by trying to understand what you would want in their situation.

B. Become incredibly interested in what other people say. React sensitively to what they say to you. Don't allow your mind to drift. Instead, ask your designated questions and try to summarize what they've said to you. That way, they understand that they've been heard.

3. BEGIN TO READ BODY LANGUAGE.

As aforementioned, body language is a full sixty percent of communication. When you begin to read between the words people say, you are truly communicating. Observe facial expressions, and try to get at the deep truth of a situation. Also, attempt to listen to people's tone of voice in order to understand if they're stressed, angry, or sad. So much about them is revealed.

4. UNDERSTAND HOW YOU AFFECT OTHER PEOPLE.

Emotional intelligence brings understanding of other people's emotions; however, you must further understand how your behaviors and emotions affect other people. For example, do you tend to make people feel happy? Nervous? Upset?

A. Think about your conversation patterns and try to understand where you might need to change your habits. If you usually pick arguments or find yourself noticing people sound stressed around you, you might need to alter your behavior so that people feel more accepted around you.

B. Ask other people how they feel when they talk to you so you can truly understand.

5. PRACTICE YOUR EMOTIONAL HONESTY.

Try to communicate your emotions honestly. For example, if you say you're "all right" and say it with a frown on your face, you're not being honest. Try to be physically open with your emotions; share happiness, share unhappiness.

A. When you're being yourself, your peers can trust you a lot better. They won't trust you if you never tell them what's wrong.

B. Understand the line between over-sharing. Try to control how you react to your feelings in order not to hurt people's feelings.

Chapter 9. Emotional Intelligence: A Leap Toward a Better, More Vibrant Future

Holding a high level of emotional intelligence is far more important for your life and the surge toward a better future than perhaps anything else. Your emotional intelligence can help you better understand your own emotions so that you can reach toward your own goals, your own successes with assured strength. You can read yourself and act on those readings appropriately rather than assimilating yourself into a continuous string of "acting on a whim." You can act with intention; you can see the benefits of acting with meaning.

Furthermore, you can bring your emotional intelligence to assist other people. When you show compassion and empathy to the people around you, they'll be far more alert and ready to respond to you. They'll have the ability to work through their feelings in order to respond appropriately, as well. This feeling of compassion and companionship can help fuel many environments including work environments and school environments. When you begin to show your compassion—and others build those feelings of compassion as well—conflicts begin to resolve themselves. Different perspectives and open-mindedness will be rampant. And a more understanding world will take form.

Together with emotional intelligence, we can:

1. Create positive relationships.

2. Teach our children to respond well to their emotions and the emotions of others.

3. Work to eliminate school bullying and the feelings of exclusion.

4. Find ways to fuel creativity and open-mindedness in all areas; this, in turn, creates innovation.

5. Build a stronger, more team-oriented planet. With this in mind, we can perhaps resolve conflicts with specific conversation; we can resolve environmentally desperate situations by discussing things openly without anger. We don't have to come at everything with emotion. We can understand our interior emotions and feel how these emotions could trigger certain actions; and we can choose how to actually react to those emotions.

With presence of mind, with emotional intelligence, we can build a stronger world.

REFERENCES

Goleman, D. (1995). *Emotional intelligence.* New York: Bantam.

Mayer, J. D., Salovey, P., & Caruso, D. R. (2000). *Models of emotional intelligence.* In R. J. Sternberg (Ed.). Handbook of Intelligence (pp. 396-420). Cambridge, England: Cambridge University Press.

Payne, W.L. (1985). *A study of emotion: developing emotional intelligence; self-integration; relating to fear, pain and desire (theory, structure of reality, problem-solving, contraction/expansion, tuning in/comingout/letting go).* A Doctoral Dissertation. Cincinnati, OH: The Union For Experimenting Colleges And Universities

Salovey, P., & Mayer, J. (1990). *Emotional intelligence. Imagination, cognition, and personality,* 9(3), 185-211.

ABOUT THE AUTHOR

My mission with this is to be able to help inspire and change the world, one reader at a time.

I want to provide the most amazing life tools that anyone can apply into their lives. It doesn't matter whether you have hit rock bottom in your life or your life is amazing and you want to keep taking it to another level.

If you are like me, then you are probably looking to become the best version of yourself. You are likely not to settle for an okay life. You want to live an extraordinary life. Not only to be filled within but also to contribute to society.

I been studying and applying psychology for over 5 years and I have met a lot of interesting people along the way. With these writings I want to keep inspiring others to change for the better.

OTHER BOOKS BY JONNY BELL

Spirituality: A Practical Guide to Spiritual Awakening: A Journey of Self-Awareness and Spiritual Growth

Sociology: A Practical Understanding of Why We Do What We Do

Personal Transformation: A Practical Guide To Unleash Your True Potential: Achieve Self Mastery In Every Area...

ONE LAST THING...

If you enjoyed this book or found it useful I'd be very grateful if you'd post a short review on Amazon. Your support really does make a difference and I read all the reviews personally so I can get your feedback and make this book even better.

Thanks again for your support!

Made in the USA
Lexington, KY
17 January 2018